boxer

understanding and
caring for your dog

Written by
Laura Clark

boxer

understanding and caring for your dog

Written by
Laura Clark

Pet Book Publishing Company

Bishton Farm, Bishton Lane, Chepstow, NP16 7LG, United Kingdom.
881 Harmony Road, Unit A, Eatonton, GA31024 United States of America.

Printed and bound in China through Printworks International.

All rights reserved. No part of this work may be reproduced, in any form
or by any means, electronic or mechanical, including photocopying,
recording or by any information storage and retrieval system, without
the prior written permission of the publisher.

Copyright © Pet Book Publishing Company 2012.

Every reasonable care has been taken in the compilation of this
publication. The Publisher and Author cannot accept liability for any
loss, damage, injury or death resulting from the keeping of Boxers by
user(s) of this publication, or from the use of any materials, equipment,
methods or information recommended in this
publication or from any errors or omissions
that may be found in the text of this
publication or that may occur at a future
date, except as expressly provided by law.

The 'he' pronoun is used throughout this
book instead of the rather impersonal 'it',
however no gender bias is intended.

ISBN: 978-1-906305-61-1
ISBN: 1-906305-61-7

Acknowledgements

The publishers would like to help the following for help with
photography: Laura Clark (Clarkenwells; John Crooks (Uftonponds);
Leigh Edgeler (Kezialeigh); and Alice Robinson (Robinsteck).

Contents

The Boxer has a worldwide fan club and owners are, quite simply, passionate about the breed. The Boxer is both friend and companion. He will be happy with you, sad with you, chill out with you – in fact, as long as he's with you, he's happy!

The Boxer comes from guarding lines and he takes his role as family protector very seriously. He adores his human pack and wants nothing more than to spend time with them and be included in all outings – even if it is only a trip in the car.

He will be alert for the approach of strangers and may be wary to begin with. He needs to work out if there is a potential threat, but once he has been reassured, he will be more than ready to welcome all comers with typical Boxer enthusiasm.

The Boxer is an active, playful dog, and he will retain his *joie de vivre* throughout his life. He does appear to have a real sense of humour; he is happy to play the clown and relishes all the attention he gets.

A Boxer needs to be loved and cared for, fed and watered. He is low maintenance in terms of coat care and dietary requirements, but he demands both mental and physical exercise. Many people think of this breed as highly energetic, with excessive exercise needs, but this is generally not the case. A Boxer will settle into most routines and, as long as he gets the opportunity to be outside and run free every day, he will keep well.

Living in a family

The Boxer has a kindly side to his nature and he gets on well with children. He will enjoy joining in their games and will keep a watch over them. However, it is important to bear in mind that a small, cuddly Boxer puppy will grow into a powerful dog, and this can be quite intimidating if good relations are not established from the start.

Children must learn how to behave so a Boxer does not get too hyped up, and the Boxer must learn to respect even the smallest members of his family pack. With careful supervision, the Boxer will soon become an integral member of the family.

Living with other animals

Sociable and fun loving, the Boxer will enjoy the company of another dog; two dogs will benefit from the additional exercise they get playing together, and they will settle more easily when you have to leave them alone.

Boxers do seem to get on especially well with other Boxers – maybe because they read each other's facial expressions and body language so easily, whereas other breeds may struggle to do this. But if you work at early introductions, a Boxer will learn to live with any breed.

Cats may be more of a problem, as the Boxer has quite a high prey drive and may find it hard to resist a cat running at speed. However, there are many instances of Boxers and cats living in harmony, particularly if a puppy and kitten are brought up together.

Small animals, such as hamsters, rabbits and guinea pigs, should be kept in secure accommodation and a Boxer should never be left alone with them. It is far better to be safe than sorry.

The all rounder

Intelligent, loyal and loving, the Boxer is the breed that has it all. He is biddable and enjoys the stimulation of training, so he is more than capable of competing with distinction in canine sports such as obedience, tracking, or agility, but he will also be content in his role as family companion and protector. The Boxer is one of the easiest breeds to live with as long as he understands his place in the family pack, and you give him the leadership he needs.

One of the great canine comedians, the Boxer enjoys life to the full.

Ancestors of the Boxer go back more than 2,000 years. Early Boxer types were used to hunt bears and boars and to fight and bait bulls. These dogs were hugely brave and had a wide jaw housed in a broad muzzle.

In the 16th and 17th centuries the dog became valued as a guard and a companion and three distinct types emerged:

- The heavy Bullenbeisser, the predecessor of the Mastiff.

- The large hound type, which became the Great Dane.

- The small Bullenbeisser, the basis for the Bulldog.

It was this third type, later crossed with the German, more elegant, type of Bulldog, that went on to become the basis for the Boxer that we know today.

The very first Boxers originated in Germany in the early 1830s. It is documented that a white English Bulldog was taken into Germany and crossed with the Bullenbeisser with the aim of producing a more elegant dog to escort horse and carriages. The female Bullenbeisser was called Flora, but the dog's name was never recorded.

The first Boxer cross was called Lechner's Boxel; he was a male and was later mated back to his mother to produce a bitch called Alt's Schecken. This bitch was later mated to a dog, named Tom, who was also a white English Bulldog. The result of this mating was Flocki, a dark brindle male with flashy white markings, born in Munich on 26 February 1895. Flocki is the first Boxer recorded in the German stud book after winning the Boxer class at a St Bernard show; he was also the first ever recorded Boxer to be shown.

The first breed standard

Further matings took place, producing some very influential dogs that provided the foundation for the breed. In January 1896, the Munich Boxer Club was formed, with its first show held in March of that year.

The entries for that show produced quite a variation in size, shape and color, so club members decided that they should try to agree a Standard for the breed. In January 1902, the first German Breed Standard – known as the Munich Standard – was adopted.

Below: White Bulldogs were crossed with early Boxers.

Developing the breed

One of the early pioneers of the breed was Friederun Stockmann and her husband, Philip. They married in 1911 and began a life-long journey to produce good-quality Boxers under their vom Dom affix.

In 1914 Philip was called to war. He took 10 of their Boxers with him into the Home Guard and set about developing the breed for the military. They were trained to find wounded soldiers, remove their tags, and then lead medical officers back to the wounded, proving the versatility of the breed.

Philip Stockman died in 1945, leaving his wife to carry on the von Dom name. Due to the difficulties of the war, Frau Stockmann had only one remaining granddaughter to carry on the line, but she succeeded, and most of today's Boxers can be traced back to her breeding.

Friederun Stockmann wrote a book called *My Life with Boxers*, which is a fascinating account of the breed's history and development. Frau Stockmann was outspoken on a number of subjects, including the envy of fellow breeders. She wrote: "If you wish to become unpopular, just buy a beautiful dog!"

The international Boxer

From its German homeland, the Boxer has spread worldwide and today it is a truly international breed. The USA led the way, importing Dampf von Dom from the Stockmanns' great von Dom kennel in Germany, and he became the first American Champion in 1915.

There are four Boxers, imported from Germany, who are largely responsible or establishing the breed in its new home. Known as 'the big four', Int. Ch. Sugurd von Dom. Ch. Lustig vom Dom, Dorian von Marienhof and Ch. Utz von Dom, were highly successful in the show ring, but it was through their offspring that their influence was truly felt. They produced generations of Champions, and were responsible for putting the American Boxer on the map.

The first British-bred Champion, Ch. Horsa of Leith Hill, was made up in 1936. He was bred from German dogs imported by breed enthusiast Mrs Cecil Sprigge.

He went on to win Best of Breed at Crufts in 1937, 1938 and 1939.

It was not until 1947 that Britain had its first Boxer bitch Champion – Ch. Panfield Serenade. Serenade was mated to her half-brother, Panfield Tango, and produced two very big winners – Panfield Ringleader and Panfield Rhythm. Between them they accumulated 17 Challenge Certificates. But it was Panfield Ringleader who went on to be the biggest influence in the UK, siring seven Champions and six other CC winners. He also had eight grandchildren that became Champions – a pretty impressive record!

As the breed developed, imports from Europe to the USA, and from the USA to Europe further enriched the gene pool. In 1950 Dutch Ch. Holger Von Germania came into the UK via the famous Wardrobes kennel owned by Mrs Connie Wiley. Marion Fairbrother and Martin Summers brought in Ch. Rainey Lane Sirrocco from the USA in 1958; he sired 13 Champions. Ivor and Marion Ward Davis of the Winuwuk kennels imported Kreyons Back in Town of Winuwuk, followed by Winuwuk Milrays Red Baron. This kennel is still one of the most influential and successful in the UK today.

Pat Heath of the Seefeld kennels bred Ch. Seefeld Holbein from a combination of Dutch imports. This dog was the only show Champion in 1960 who also qualified for working trials – proving, again, the versatility of the breed. Holbein went on to produce Ch. Seefeld Picasso, who sired 18 UK Champions and 58 Champions worldwide. This kennel has had a largely American influence in its development.

Today, there are some difference in type between the British and the American Boxers, and this is more marked with the differences in tails and ears (see page 32?). However, the essentials of this magnificent breed have stood the test of time, and the Boxer is one of the most popular breeds worldwide.

What should a Boxer look like?

The Breed Standard is a detailed description of type, size, shape, colors, movement and temperament. In the show ring, Boxers are judged against the Breed Standard, and it is the dog that, in the judge's opinion, conforms most closely to the Standard, that will win honours and be used in future breeding programs.

General appearance

The Boxer is a medium-sized, square built dog with strong bone and well developed muscles. He has a noble appearance, combining strength and agility with elegance and style.

Temperament

The correct Boxer temperament should always be considered a top priority. Bred for his guarding abilities, the Boxer is protective of his family and may be distrustful of strangers until they are properly introduced. If needed, he is capable of great courage. However, the Boxer at home with his family is loving, loyal and playful.

Head

The Boxer is known as a 'head breed', meaning that this is his most distinguishing feature. However, when assessing or judging a dog, the whole dog must be taken into account. Face on, the head should be brick-shaped rather than rounded, with the top of the head, across from ear to ear, slightly wider than the muzzle. In a young dog you would expect to see some rise of skull, sometimes even a dome on top of the head. This will flatten with growth.

Below the eyes, above the nose, is the stop, which is where the nose/muzzle join the face. This should be indented but not sunken into the head.

The muzzle should be well padded with the flews not much below the chin, with creases running down the sides of the muzzle from the root of

Points of anatomy

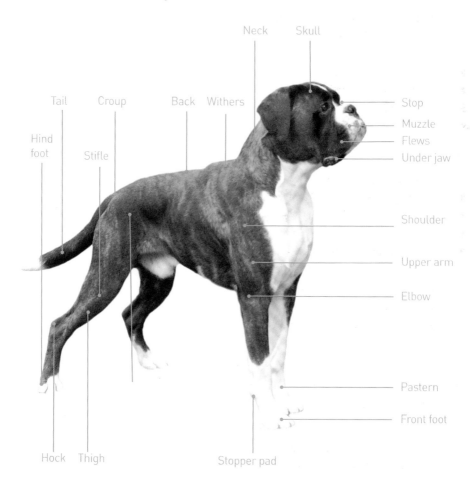

Neck

Skull

Tail

Croup

Back

Withers

Stop

Muzzle

Flews

Under jaw

Hind foot

Stifle

Shoulder

Upper arm

Elbow

Pastern

Front foot

Hock

Thigh

Stopper pad

the nose. The tip of the nose should be set slightly higher than the root.

The muzzle should be of good width, and the lower jaw should be undershot – i.e. slightly longer than the top jaw. There should be four large canine teeth, two at the top and two at the bottom, set wide apart, and six good-sized incisor teeth set in a straight row on the bottom jaw and slightly curved on the top jaw. In the middle are the premolars and at the back of the jaw the larger molars. A total of 42 teeth is normal.

The Boxer's undershot jaw differs from many other breeds that have a scissor bite. Remember, the Boxer jaw was originally designed for gripping on to prey, unlike the scissor bite which is designed for ripping through meat. The undershot jaw does not normally present the Boxer with any eating problems.

Ears

These should be a good size, and they should reach down approximately one-third to half of the face. They should lie flat and face forward, not on the side of the head. In the USA, show dogs sometimes have their ears cropped, which gives the face a very different expression (see page 32).

Eyes

These should be round and quite large but not bulging, looking straight ahead not on the sides of the head. Above the eyes should be quite clean – i.e. not overly wrinkled; wrinkles should show when the dog is alert, but should not be heavy over the eyes. The eyes should be a dark brown color and the rims need to be pigmented – i.e. dark in color, not pale or white.

The expression in the Boxer's eyes is so revealing. It should be alert, bold, confident, never aggressive, making the dog appear interested and wanting to please.

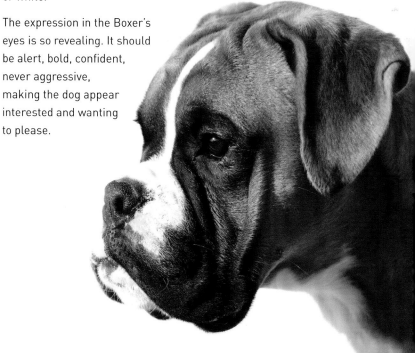

Below: The Boxer is known as a 'head breed'.

Neck

The neck needs to be of good length and well muscled. It should not be long and thin like a swan, but should add some elegance to the picture. There should be a distinctly marked nape to the neck, with an elegant arch down to the withers, fitting well into laid-back shoulders.

Forequarters

The shoulders should be long and sloping, attached at a right angle to a long upper arm. The forearms are straight, long and well muscled. The pasterns are short and slightly slanted. The front feet should be cat-like with well-arched toes and hard pads.

Hindquarters

These should be strong, well muscled, with plenty of power to drive. The upper and lower thighs should be long and well muscled with good angulation, and no exaggeration. The hock joints are clean, with strong rear pads.

Tail

Traditionally the Boxer was docked but this is now banned in many countries. The natural tail is usually long, carried upward when moving or excited, often lower when eating, resting or uneasy about something. In the USA show dogs still have their tails docked.

Movement

The Boxer should have a driving movement, with the power coming from the rear. In order to have good movement the dog must be correctly constructed. Always remember that the Boxer is a working dog and, if required, should be able to do a day's work. It is therefore important to breed for the bone and construction that would make this possible.

Coat and color

The coat should be glossy, short and tight to the body. The acceptable colors are fawn, often called red, and brindle. White markings are acceptable but must not exceed one-third of the entire coat. White Boxers do crop up in litters, but they are not eligible for the show ring and should not be bred from.

Tops and tails

The Boxer was bred for his noble good looks as well as for his temperament. However, changes in legislation have affected his appearance more than most breeds.

Ears

The very first Boxers had cropped ears, and this practice continued for much of the breed's history in North America and Germany, although the UK has promoted natural ears in all breeds. Ear cropping is now banned in many countries, although they are still seen in the American show ring.

The stipulation in the American Breed Standard is for the ears to be cut long and tapering and raised when the dog is alert. This gives the Boxer a completely different expression, and judges in the USA have to assess dogs with cropped ears and uncropped ears alongside each other, as both types are permitted.

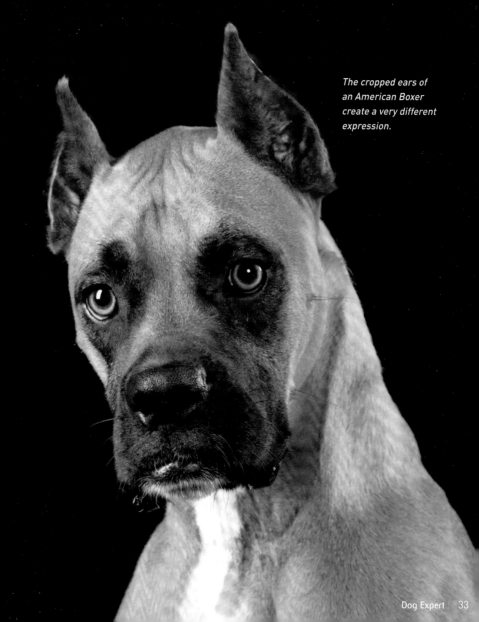

The cropped ears of an American Boxer create a very different expression.

Tails

The Boxer was originally designed to have his tail docked, and it is only relatively recently that docking has been criticized and is now banned in most European countries. In the USA show dogs are still exhibited with docked tails and, in fact, the American Breed Standard states that an undocked tail should be severely penalized.

In countries where docking is banned, the natural tail can vary enormously. Some tails are held up high, some curl over the back, some are straight up or held out horizontally. There is also a range of different lengths and thicknesses within the breed. This causes breeders much consternation, as there is little guidance on what is now considered to be 'correct' for the breed.

Bobtail Boxers

The idea of developing a naturally short tail in the Boxer was put into practice in the early 1990s, and is attributed to Dr Bruce Cattanach, a geneticist and also a keen and successful Boxer breeder.

He has established generations of bobtail Boxers, who have achieved some success in the show ring.

Docking is now illegal in the UK, and breeders are striving to establish a tail and tail carriage that is typical for the breed.

It is possible to breed a bob-tailed Boxer.

What do you want from your Boxer?

Before you make the commitment to own a Boxer, you should work out exactly what you want from your dog, and whether a Boxer is truly suitable for your lifestyle.

Responsible breeders will quiz you about your experience and your expectations, as they want to be sure that a prospective buyer can give a puppy all he needs. You need to be clear about what you want the dog for – do you want a companion, a show dog, a working dog, or a dog to breed from?

Companion dogs

The Boxer is a superb companion and will fit in with many different types of households. However, he is strong and lively, and may be too much for

older people, particularly if they have any physical disabilities. For the same reason, the Boxer may not be best suited to a family with very small children. His temperament is impeccable, but unless he is well trained, he may be a little too boisterous, particularly when he is growing up.

As we have seen, this is a breed that requires firm handling and so this may be challenging if you have never owned a dog before.

Show dogs

Showing is an addictive pastime, and if this is the sport for you, your life will soon be taken over by the season's fixtures. It is highly competitive at the top level and if you are to have any chance of success you need to go to a reputable breeder who has produced some top winners in the ring.

It is very important that the breeder knows of your intentions so they can pick out a puppy with show potential. Remember, there are no guarantees; a puppy can change a great deal during the first 12 months of his life, and you can only go on how he looks at around eight weeks of age.

Working dogs

Do you have ambitions to get involved on one of the canine sports, such as competitive obedience, agility or tracking? With the right training, the Boxer is successful in all these fields. He is a highly intelligent dog that was bred to work, so if you have the time and the patience, you could become a winning partnership.

Breeding stock

Breeding is a highly specialised business and should only be undertaken by those who have a true vocation to serve the breed and produce puppies of the highest quality. If you are new to the breed, you need to discuss your plans with experienced breeders, and carry out detailed research before embarking on such a project.

What does your Boxer want from you?

At the same time as you are considering what you want from your Boxer, you should also be considering if you can provide a suitable home and cater for his specific needs.

Finance

You need to have the finances available to be able to provide him with good-quality food, equipment, and health care. You may wish to consider insurance for your dog, or just save a regular amount each month in case you need a visit to the vet. In any event, you will need to pay for vaccinations initially and then annually, plus worming and flea treatment on a regular basis.

If you plan to go on holiday without your Boxer, you will need to make suitable arrangements which may involve paying boarding kennels.

Time

A Boxer is a loyal member of the family and he needs to be with his people. You need to commit to spending time with him, and if you go to work, you need to find someone who can care for him in your absence. A dog should never be left for longer than four hours at a time – and this is too long for a growing puppy. So think and plan carefully before deciding you can take on a Boxer.

Exercise

A Boxer needs mental and physical exercise; he needs some lead walking and some off-lead running to keep him in good shape. While he is still growing, exercise should be limited to protect his vulnerable joints, but in adulthood a Boxer will thrive on a regime of daily, varied walks where he can see new sights and investigate interesting scents.

A place in the family

When you take on a Boxer, it is important that you think about the behavior you want from your dog. You need to work out the dog's place in your family, and consider what his role will be. By nature, a Boxer wants to fit into your pack, but if he sees a gap in the leadership, he may challenge for that place.

Socialization and training

A Boxer does not come ready-made as a polite, well-behaved individual, fitting in with family life. He has to be taught the house rules be trained in basic obedience and socialized with other people and with other dogs so that he reacts calmly and confidently in all situations. This requires a considerable amount of time but it is of paramount importance if you want your Boxer to become a model canine citizen.

Before arranging to see a litter of puppies, you need to narrow your choice so the breeder knows exactly what you are looking for.

Male or female?

Whether you choose a male or a female is a matter of personal preference, but there are a few points to bear in mind.

The temperaments of the two sexes can be quite different and often people will stick to what they have had before. However, both have their pros and cons. A bitch is smaller and possibly easier to handle, but not necessarily easier to train. A male, on the other hand, is more loyal and better focused when training, but he is larger, stronger and, in his adolescence, he may be mischievous and more challenging in his behavior.

You may decide to have your dog neutered, which is a sensible option if you do not want to get involved in breeding. A dog can be neutered from six months of age. Vets and breeders will have their own ideas about the best time for neutering, so it is best to seek advice.

What color?

You may have set your heart on a color – and this may also have a bearing on the price. Basically, your choice is: red, brindle, red and white, brindle and white, or white. Animals may be referred to as "flashy" or "solid"; this refers to the color around the face, mask, muzzle, chest and feet. A flashy dog will have white markings on a dark background, and this type will command the highest price, as they are more popular in the show ring.

White puppies are usually sold for less money, as they cannot be shown or bred from, although they do make great pets. However, there is another, more serious consideration; white puppies are prone to deafness, and this should be discussed with the breeder before a sale is made.

White Boxers make fabulous pets but check with the breeder as they are prone to deafness.

More than one?

Puppies are irresistible, so much so that you might be tempted to take on two pups from the same litter. However, you will end up giving yourself more than double the workload, particularly when it comes to training. In this situation, even getting the puppies to respond to their own names is more difficult, and any issues regarding health or temperament will be exacerbated.

It is true that puppies will play together and keep each other company but, on the whole, I think it is advisable to wait until your first Boxer is grown up – at least 18 months old – before taking on a second.

Older dogs

It may suit your lifestyle to miss
out on the puppy stage and take
on an older dog. Sometimes
a breeder may have older dogs
available – a puppy may not have
fulfilled his show potential, or a female
may have finished her breeding career.

In this situation, the breeder may feel
the dog will be happier as a much-
loved family companion rather than
living in a multi-dog household.

Rescued dogs

You may decide to take on a rescued Boxer, giving a dog another chance to find a loving permanent home. Many of the breed clubs run rescue schemes, and the big all-breed rescue charities are always looking for new and reliable owners.

There are many dogs who end up in rescue through no fault of their own – marital break up, moving home, or the arrival of a new baby are the most common reasons why dogs need to be rehomed. However, there may be some Boxers who have not received the training and socialization that is so important with this breed and, as a result, they may have some behavioral problems.

If you plan to take on a rescued Boxer, find out as much as you can about the dog's background to make sure you can cope. It is no kindness to rehome a Boxer, only to hand it back because his behavior is too challenging for you.

Sourcing a puppy

Where to buy? There are lots of options available, but some are far better than others. So, do not just buy the first puppy you see or hear about.

Many puppies are advertised on the Internet and photos of Boxer puppies (or any other breed for that matter) will look adorable – but not every adorable puppy grows into a healthy and well-adjusted adult. The Internet is a good source of information, but the recommended sites are those run by national Kennel Clubs, where you will also find advice about choosing a puppy and finding a reputable breeder. Breed clubs may be able to put you in touch with local breeders in your area, or, indeed, if you know the name or affix of a particular breeder, they may they have their own website. But this alone does not make them a reputable breeder.

Be wary of newspapers with advertisements for domestic pets. The adverts may be free, or very cheap, which may attract the novice breeder. Specialist dog publications may be a better bet, but there are no guarantees. Recommendations from people who have already bought from a particular breeder are usually reliable.

When looking for a Boxer, make sure you know what you want, how much you are willing to pay, and ensure you have researched the health and requirements of the Boxer breed.

Puppy farms

Puppy farms should be avoided at all costs. A puppy farm is a place where many puppies are bred and there are usually, but not necessarily, many different breeds. The puppies are bred for financial gain, with little or no regard for the well-being of the mother or the puppies in the long term.

Do not buy a puppy because you feel sorry for him. You run the risk of taking on a sickly puppy that will cost you a fortune in vet bills, and may well end in heartbreak.

Kennel Clubs

In order to encourage and promote responsible breeders, a number of national Kennel Clubs now run accreditation schemes – the American Kennel Club recognizes Breeders of Merit, the UK has the Assured Breeders Scheme.

The schemes vary in minor details but the aim is to encourage breeders to follow a recognized code of practice, which is in the interests of the breed. The following guidelines apply:

- All breeding stock must be Kennel Club registered.

- Breeders should hand over registration documents at the time of sale, or soon afterwards, and explain fully any endorsements.

- Breeders must follow KC policy regarding the age of the breeding bitch and the number of litters she may produce.

Below: Do not fall into the trap of buying a puppy because your feel sorry for him.

- Breeding stock must be permanently identified by microchip, DNA or tattoo.

- Breeders must use health-screening schemes relevant to the breed where available.

- Breeders must socialize the puppies and provide written advice on feeding, on-going training, socialization, worming and vaccinations.

- Breeders must provide reasonable after-sales telephone advice.

- Breeders must draw up a contract of sale for each puppy.

In addition to the above, it is expected that the breeder will employ high standards of cleanliness and management when rearing the puppies, taking good care of the mother, and having the best interests of the animals at heart.

The schemes need further development, particularly with regard to policing, but the majority of responsible breeders see the benefits for the breed as a whole.

The Kennel Club provides no guarantee for puppies sold by members of the scheme, so it is still your responsibility to ask all the right questions and be sure that you are happy with what you see and what you are told by the breeder.

Facing page: You need to find a breeder with a reputation for producing sound, healthy puppies that are typical of the breed.

Health issues

Boxers have a number of health issues to be considered, and so you need to take sensible precautions to ensure the puppy that you buy has had the best start in life.

The major concerns within the Boxer breed are cancer and two types of heart disease: aortic stenosis and cardiomyopathy.

For more information on inherited and breed-disposed disorders, see page 180.

You should be aware of health issues that affect the breed.

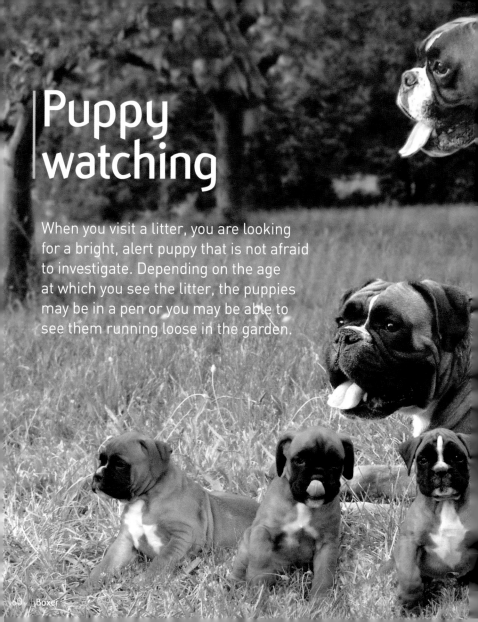

Puppy watching

When you visit a litter, you are looking for a bright, alert puppy that is not afraid to investigate. Depending on the age at which you see the litter, the puppies may be in a pen or you may be able to see them running loose in the garden.

Most breeders will not allow visitors until the puppies are at least four weeks, but the best time is about six weeks, when the puppies have begun playing and start showing their personalities. You should be able to handle the puppies and observe them in their home environment.

You should be able to see the mother with her puppies to get an idea of the temperament the puppies are likely to inherit. It is unlikely that the stud dog (the father of the litter) will be living on the premises as breeders often have to travel considerable distances to find the perfect match. However, you should be able to see photos of him, and be given a chance to look at his pedigree and show record.

Assessing a puppy

If you are looking for a pet, temperament and health are the priorities. You will need to have established if both the parents have been heart tested, and then you can begin to look at the pups.

- Look for bright, clear eyes with no discharge.

- Check inside the ears; they should be clean with no signs of redness or sores.

- The coat should be shiny and lying flat to the body.

- The puppy should well covered, i.e. you should not be able to see ribs and pin bones, and there should be plenty of skin for the puppy to grow into.

- Look for strong, round bone in the forelegs and good-sized, tight, cat-like feet.

- There should be good degree of angulation in the hock, with the tail looking like an extension of the spine.

Watch the puppies playing together to assess their temperaments. At around six weeks they can be very vocal and will scrap among themselves. This is just a way of learning how to communicate and finding out what is accepted by others in the pack. The mother may also be involved in this process and, indeed, it is her job to put the puppies in their place if they are overstepping the mark.

I believe it is important for all the family to meet the puppy before he goes home. If young children are afraid of the puppy at this stage, it could be tricky later, in which case you should consider waiting until the children are older and more confident. Most breeders will be happy for you to take photos and visit again as the pups get older. Never be afraid to ask questions when you visit; it is important that you are able to discuss any issues, concerns or plans you have.

Working puppy

If you want your Boxer to work in obedience, agility, working trials or tracking, temperament is all-important. You should be looking for a puppy with an out-going, inquisitive personality.

It is not always easy to assess temperament at an early age. I was once told that what you see at six weeks is what you get, and, in terms of body shape, this has rung true. However, personality and temperament develop over time and are more dependent on the puppy's early life experiences.

Below: Are you interested in working your Boxer?

Show puppy

Looking for a show puppy is a highly specialised business and, generally, you will be acting on advice from the breeder. If a puppy is likely to be shown in the ring, the breeder will be anxious to keep their reputation intact and will help you choose a puppy with maximum potential. Ideally, take someone with you that you trust and who knows about showing. Two heads are better than one!

When buying your first show puppy, do not have massive expectations, as there is a lot to learn. In the first six months before you can show the puppy there are many things to consider in terms of your learning and the pup's development. I was once told that there is a 10-year apprenticeship before you can really expect to do much winning. Patience, determination and a willingness to learn are the key points.

In summary

Do some research before you embark on this important journey. Health and temperament are the main factors you must consider, as well as ensuring that all the family are committed and ready for bringing a Boxer into your home. Remember: the dog you take home is a dog for life!

The breeder will help you to evaluate a puppy with show potential.

Preparation is very important before you bring your new dog home. There is little difference between bringing a puppy or an older dog at this stage, as the same things need to be considered.

The garden

Check that the garden boundaries are safe for the new arrival. Ensure there are no gaps in the fencing that a puppy can escape through and that any other garden features, such as a pond, are made safe. A pond can be a death trap for a puppy. I find the best way is to imagine you are bringing a small child into the garden and ask yourself if it would be safe for them.

Boxers are capable jumpers and so a fence needs to be sturdy and at least 1.5 m (around 5 ft), preferably higher. Gates need to be sturdy with a lock and fastening that cannot be opened by an intelligent dog.

Be aware of chemicals you may have in your garden, such as fertiliser for the lawn, weed or ant killer. All of these, if eaten by a small puppy, could be fatal. Keep all toxic substances in a secure place, well out of reach. Rat poison and slug pellets are particularly dangerous. You will also need to be sure that you have no plants in the garden that are toxic to dogs; you can find a full list on the internet.

In the home

Safety also needs to be considered in the home. Look around and ask yourself what mischief a puppy could get up to and what he could chew. Electric cables are prime candidates, so these should be safely secured where a puppy cannot reach them. Anything breakable, such as glass or china, is very dangerous, as, once broken, a puppy could tread on sharp pieces, or even swallow them. House plants also need to be out of reach, as, even if they are not poisonous, they will very likely upset a puppy's tummy.

Sleeping quarters

Your puppy will want a place to sleep or rest to call his own. This should be somewhere that is warm and safe with no drafts. It is often advisable to set up a bed or a crate in the kitchen, or a secure area that will be easy to clean, such as a utility room.

Many people do not like the idea of a crate for the dog to sleep in. However, the dog just sees it as his place and will willingly spend time there once initially trained to do so. The big advantage is that it keeps your puppy safe overnight and at other times when you cannot supervise him.

When your Boxer is fully grown, the crate can also be useful if he has been accustomed to it from puppyhood. For example, if your Boxer needs an operation or is ill and must be rested, he will settle in his crate.

Sometimes you will have visitors who are nervous or even afraid of dogs, especially a big Boxer, so, again, it is useful to have a space where the dog can be both secure and comfortable.

A crate is also the safest way to travel with your dog, protecting the dog and your car! They are available in many shapes and sizes and I would strongly recommend their use.

When using a crate, ensure you buy one big enough to last until the dog is an adult. While he is still a new puppy you will have space in the crate to put newspaper at one end and the bed at the other, which will help the house-training process. During the day put puppy in his crate for a while to rest, then let him out, allowing him time outside to relieve himself and then he can come back in the house. You will find that the puppy or older dog will soon settle into his new home and will come and go from the crate as he chooses.

Finding a vet

If you do not know of a local veterinary practice, look for one close to home that also deals with its own emergency calls and is happy to have Boxers on its books.

The puppy or any new arrival really should be checked over by a vet as soon as possible to give you peace of mind and also to introduce him to the vet. Animals need not be afraid of the vet, so the more enjoyable visits you can have, the better. If an

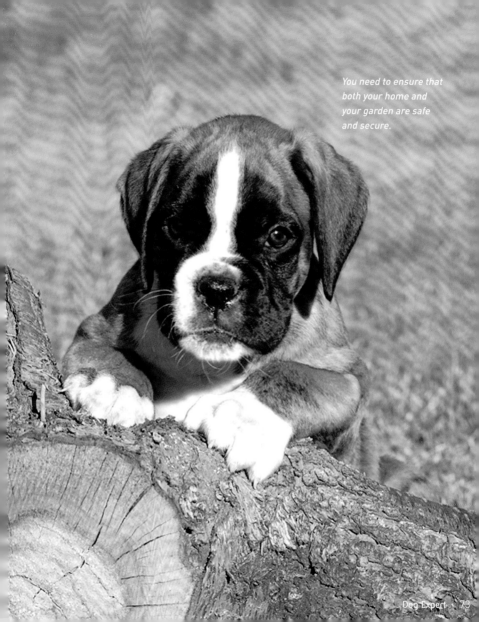

You need to ensure that both your home and your garden are safe and secure.

emergency arises, it is important that the vet is able to handle your dog.

The vet will need to see any previous vaccination record and will register all the details both for you and the dog. He or she will discuss with you feeding, worming, flea treatment, and probably microchipping, at the vaccination visit.

See Health Care, page 154

Buying equipment

You may want to purchase all you need in advance of the new arrival. However, there are some essential buys and often things that can wait:

Collar

This will need to be replaced as the puppy grows, so a grand, leather collar will probably be wasted; wait until the puppy is older and has done most of his growing.

A nylon collar with a click fastening is recommended, and it is easily washed, not too expensive and safe. When your Boxer is away from home, he should wear a collar at all times with a name and contact number on it.

Lead

Often a lead is bought to match the collar, but make sure your choice is practical. A first puppy lead can be relatively lightweight, and, if it is made of nylon, it can be washed. However, as your Boxer grows, it is important to upgrade his lead.

I would recommend a strong lead, which is quite long so that the dog can walk out in front of you, but easy to shorten when closer heelwork is required. You can buy a lead made of nylon, leather or rope – the choice is up to you.

Bedding

Your puppy will need a warm, safe bed that is big enough to allow for growing room. Be aware that this first bed may get trashed so don't spend too much on it. The bedding needs to be easily washed and dried. Most pet shops sell a wide range of beds to suit all sizes and budgets.

Bowls

There are plenty to choose from, and as long as the dog can easily get his head in to eat, it will be big enough. But you also need to think of the safety aspect. A ceramic bowl can be easily broken and a plastic bowl will be chewed. Stainless-steel bowls are best, as they are durable and easy to keep clean. Buy two - one for food and one for water.

Toys

Maybe not essential, but a puppy and an adult Boxer will certainly enjoy them! Get one or two toys to start with, and see what your Boxer likes most before buying more.

When choosing toys, safety is the top priority. There are masses of dog toys on the market today, but many can be highly dangerous if they are chewed and swallowed. If the toy is soft and can be destroyed, ensure that the dog is always supervised, as small parts of the toy may be swallowed and the stuffing may be eaten. Solid, hard plastic and rubber toys are the best, as even a Boxer finds it hard to chew through them.

If you want your Boxer to play with a ball, it must be larger than a tennis ball, as an adult Boxer can swallow a small ball whole. Do not allow the puppy to chew and play with old shoes or slippers; they will get destroyed and can be harmful to the dog if parts are swallowed – and, remember, the dog will not know the difference between old and new!

Grooming equipment

In your grooming kit you will need the following:

- A towel to dry and rub off mud.

- A brush to groom the coat.

- A duster type cloth or mitt to polish the coat.

- Wipes to keep the eyes and ears clean. If your Boxer is very wrinkled, the creases down the face or over the nose may also need attention.

- Later on you can progress to clipping your puppy's nails with small clippers or baby scissors. Ask the breeder or a vet to show you how to do this.

- Toothbrush and toothpaste to clean teeth regularly (many vets and retailers in the animal industry will recommend cleaning teeth, some breeders will not). Dental treatment is expensive and usually involves a general anesthetic.

ID

Your Boxer should have an ID disc attached to his collar or you can get contact details embroidered on to the collar. However, permanent ID such as microchipping and tattooing is a good idea. Both methods are quick and relatively painless, and can be carried out by a suitably qualified person at six to eight weeks.

*Facing page:
You may want to consider a permanent form of ID in addition to an engraved disc on the collar.*

Setting in

When collecting your puppy, make sure you leave enough time for him to become accustomed to his new environment before bed-time.

He will need to explore the garden, discover where his sleeping quarters are located, and he will also need feeding. If he does not eat all his food to begin with, do not worry. A puppy has so much to get used to as he settles in his new home, he may lose his appetite for the first few meals.

For information on feeding, see Chapter Four: Caring for your Boxer.

Meeting the family

All the family will be excited to meet the new arrival, but this is a very daunting experience for a puppy, so try not to overwhelm him. Allow the puppy to go outside and relieve himself, and then take him into one room – maybe the kitchen. Watch and observe him in his new environment; you will begin to see his temperament emerging, and you will be able to

imagine just how much fun you are going to have together! Stay with your puppy as much as possible, talk to him and reassure him, gradually building a rapport and trust.

If you have children, try to keep them as calm as possible. They can have all the fun they like in the weeks and years to come, but go a little easy, especially if the Boxer is a puppy or is being rehomed from a completely different environment. The children must understand that the puppy is not a toy and must be treated with respect. The language the child uses must be the same as the one you use, as confusion will only make training more difficult.

Be especially careful with very young children who want to pick up the puppy – a pup is very wriggly and can be easily dropped. The best approach is to ask the child to sit on the floor to cuddle the pup, so there is less risk of damage to the puppy. The puppy should also be discouraged from play-biting right from the start.

Puppies play-bite as they interact with their siblings and will yelp if the play gets too rough. This teaches them to inhibit this type of behavior. In the same way, if your puppy bites, let him know that it hurts by crying out "Ouch" in a high-pitched tone of

voice, and then introduce a command to prevent it happening again.

I say "No" and then place the flat of my hand toward the puppy so it is difficult for him to bite again. If the puppy inhibits his behavior and stops biting, give him a treat, making sure he takes it gently rather than snatching it. Say "Gently" when giving the treat, and hesitate slightly before allowing the puppy to take it. Give lots of verbal praise, using a warm, encouraging tone of voice.

Never leave small children unsupervised with a dog you do not know well; even a puppy could do some damage, so always exercise caution when children are involved.

Family pets

If you have other pets in your family, introduce them one at a time. If you have an adult dog, allow him to meet the new arrival in the garden where they will have more space and freedom to get to know each other.

Initial interactions should be closely supervised; you must not allow an older dog to completely overpower a puppy, so you may need to exercise a little control.

Give your puppy and older dog a chance to establish their own relationship.

However, it is also important that the dogs are allowed to establish their own relationship. Give them space to do this in the garden and when you are out walking and they can go off-lead together. At home, make sure you do not favour either dog. A jealous dog can become protective of one member of the family; he may try to guard his food and toys, and he may growl or even show his teeth before lunging at the other dog. This situation is much less likely to arise if pets are well socialized as puppies, which is why it is so important to get these things right in the first six months.

Your dogs should be able to share beds and toys, but take extra care at meal times. Feed each dog in a separate bowl in his own special place, and supervised if necessary.

If you have a cat, take care on the first meetings so neither the puppy nor the cat gets too much of a shock. You will need to be vigilant for the first few months as they get used to each other, for a cat can do a lot of damage – especially to a puppy's eyes – if he suddenly strikes out.

The first night

When you first take the puppy home, he
will miss his littermates and may cry
or even howl at night after you
have put the lights out and gone
to bed. The best way to deal
with this is as though you were
caring for a child. Basically,
the puppy wants your attention.
Each time you give it, the puppy
has more reason to cry the next time
because he gets what he wants.

I know it is tough, but it really is best to ignore your puppy for a few nights until he learns that crying gets him nowhere, so he may as well settle down. If you give in to this behavior at the start, you may find yourself spending the next 10 years sharing your bed with a Boxer!

House rules

You must start as you mean to go on. You need to establish the house rules and stick to them so your Boxer understands what is, and what is not, allowed. For example, you need to decide if the puppy is going to be allowed to share the furniture with you. If the answer to this question is no, do not allow it from the start. It is much harder to change habits than to not allow them to develop in the first place – remember, in just four months this puppy will be much bigger, and by a year old he could take up the whole sofa!

If the dog is not to be allowed upstairs, a stair gate is the easiest option. Incidentally, going up and down stairs of any kind is not encouraged, as it may prove damaging on puppy joints, so make sure you restrict this type of exertion.

Many new owners fall into the trap of treating the new arrival as a baby, excusing bad behavior because the puppy is so sweet. It does not take

long before the puppy is running the show and a six-month-old Boxer is not easy to re-educate. Remember, your Boxer needs to know who the leader is; if this is clear, he will follow willingly.

What you do with your Boxer in the first few days and weeks will have a bearing on the rest of his life with you. So start as you mean to go on, ensuring both your dog and your family know the rules and stick to them.

House training

This is a very important early lesson. Generally, puppies like to be clean, so it is a matter of establishing a routine. A puppy's outlook on where to go to the toilet may be influenced by his very early upbringing and the facilities that he and his littermates had to use. In most cases this is a positive thing, and most puppies will instinctively want to keep their sleeping quarters clean.

If you want your puppy to use a specific area of the garden, take him to the same spot every time you go out, and praise him when he performs. Your puppy will soon learn that this is his toilet area, and you can help by introducing a command, such as "Busy", so he connects the word with the desired action. This may take a little patience, but it is worthwhile.

Puppies are creatures of habit, so it is easy to work out when you should take your puppy out into the garden to relieve himself. Take him out at the following times:

- First thing in the morning

- After mealtimes

- After waking from a nap

- After a play session

- Last thing at night.

Do not expect a young puppy to go for longer than two hours before taking him outside, as he will need to relieve himself frequently. Your patience is required, but it really is worth taking the time to get it right now.

If you let your puppy out and leave him to it, you will miss the opportunity to reward him for doing what you want. He may get distracted and not go, so when he comes back into the house, he may then have an accident.

If your puppy has an accident, always ask yourself: did I give him enough opportunity? What should I do differently? Do not scold your puppy – and never rub his nose in the mess. Education is the answer and this can only be achieved through patience.

If you are experiencing difficulties with house training, try using some newspaper or buy some puppy training pads. Encourage the puppy to go on the paper and move it closer and closer to the door. Reduce food and fluid intake after 7pm to help your puppy to go through the night.

Remember the golden rules: be vigilant, praise your puppy lavishly when he gets it right, and do not chastise him for making mistakes – particularly as it will usually be your fault!

If you establish a routine of taking your puppy out at regular intervals, he will soon learn to be clean in the house.

Choosing a diet

Providing a well-balanced, good-quality diet is of paramount importance, as this is the key to owning a fit, healthy dog. There are lots of different diets to choose from, and you will need to weigh up convenience, availability and, most importantly, what is best for your Boxer.

Complete diet

This comes in the form of dried food and it is scientifically formulated to cater for all your dog's nutritional needs. It is the modern, most popular, approach to feeding, and it is certainly the most convenient.

There are many brands of kibble available and most offer life-stage foods, such as puppy, junior, adult and senior. There are also special diets for bitches in whelp, for working dogs, and prescription diets for

Facing page: You need to find a diet that will suit your Boxer's age and liefestyle.

weight control, and other health-related conditions.

Which kibble is best? This is a difficult question, but the best plan is to seek advice from your puppy's breeder or other breeders that have experience of different makes.

To help avoid bloat (see page 183) I soak kibble in warm water.

Canned food

This is not a complete food and needs to be served with a mixer. It usually has a high moisture content. Read the label carefully so you are aware of the ingredients and, remember, what you put in will affect what comes out.

Canned food should be served with a good proportion of biscuit to aid digestion and to promote dental health.

Traditional

The BARF diet (which stands for Biologically Appropriate Raw Food) is about providing the dog with a food that is very close to a natural diet if he were in the wild. It comprises raw meat, bones, offal, fat, and vegetable matter.

Those who use it believe it is healthier for the Boxer than manufactured food. However, this diet can be time-consuming to prepare and you need to ensure that your dog is getting all the nutrients he needs.

Further information regarding the BARF diet can be found on numerous websites.

Changing Diet

There may be a time when you need to change your Boxer's diet. Perhaps you have difficulty getting hold of a particular brand, or you may find the food is not suiting your dog.

In this situation, you need to introduce the new food gradually, over seven to 10 days, adding a little more of the new food as your dog becomes accustomed to it. A sudden change of diet will lead to gastric upset.

Fresh water

Whatever type of diet you choose, you must ensure that fresh, clean drinking water is available at all times.

Dog Treats

Treats should only be used when your dog has done well in training or has behaved particularly well in a difficult situation. Your Boxer should learn to work for his treats and not expect them on a routine basis. Favorite treats include cheese, sausage, or liver.

Alternatively, you can buy a huge variety of manufactured small treats for training, which are very useful and not as messy as fresh foods.

Avoid manufactured treats that have too many additives. Do not feed sweet biscuits, buttered toast, fatty bacon, or chocolate, which is toxic to dogs.

Bones and chews

Manufactured bones and chews are loved by most dogs, but they often prove dangerous if the dog is left unsupervised. I prefer giving biscuit bones rather than hide chews, which become soft and glue-like, and can be swallowed. The result can be an irritated gut or, worse, a blockage that could have lethal consequences. If you give your dog hide chews, remove them before they become soft and easy to swallow.

Puppy diet

Correct feeding can be the key to rearing a healthy dog. As a puppy, your Boxer will need good-quality food, fed up to four times a day. He will need the right combination of proteins, carbohydrates, fats, vitamins and minerals so that he fulfils his growth potential.

The big advantage of feeding a complete diet, is that you can be confident that it provides for all nutritional needs and does not need supplementing. However, this type of diet tends to lack taste and texture, and I like to add some form of meat to make the meal more appetizing.

Recommended puppy diet (eight weeks plus)

- **Breakfast:** Up to half a scoop of kibble (start with about 1.7-2.8 ounces/50-80 grams), mixed with a little meat – this could be tinned or frozen tripe, canned food, fresh mince, fresh chicken, tuna (not in any kind of oil) or white fish with no bones. Fresh meat should be cooked before serving.

  Always consider healthy options, and make sure you increase the amount of food as the puppy grows.

- **Lunch:** A couple of scrambled eggs, some grated cheese, with maybe a slice of wholemeal bread, soaked in warm water.

- **Dinner:** As breakfast.

- **Supper:** Cereal and warm milk, rice pudding or porridge.

By the time your puppy is four to five months old, you can drop the supper; by six months, you can cut out the lunch. Show and working stock may continue with more mealtimes for a longer period. If your puppy seems underweight, carry on with the lunch until he is up to the correct weight – take advice from your puppy's breeder or vet.

Adult diet

I prefer to feed my dogs twice a day, but they can do just as well if fed only once.

Recommended adult diet

- **Breakfast and dinner:** Up to a whole scoop of kibble, 6-7 oz (180-200 g), soaked and cooled, mixed with canned or frozen tripe, canned or fresh meat, as for a puppy.

- For variety you can add boiled rice, plain cooked pasta, gravy, some well-cooked vegetables, grated cheese, or scrambled egg, all in moderation. Be aware that some of these may not agree with your dog and could cause an upset tummy.

Caring for your Boxer

The Boxer is a low-maintenance breed, particularly in relation to grooming, but make sure you check your dog on a regular basis so you can pick up signs of trouble at an early stage.

Coat care

The Boxer's coat should shine and lie flat; it should be soft to the touch and not smell.

Groom through the coat regularly with a soft brush; you can use a hand glove to remove mud if necessary and it is also useful for removing dead hair when your Boxer is shedding his coat. Finish off by smoothing the coat with a cloth to polish the surface using the natural oils in the coat, and it should be gleaming!

The Boxer can be a little prone to sensitive skin, which is often helped by providing a good-quality

diet. Human skin supplements may be of use, but always take veterinary advice before going down this route. I have found that evening primrose and cod liver oil are beneficial. However, if you spot red or sore patches, you should book a visit to the vet.

Do not bath your Boxer more than necessary, as it removes the natural oils in the coat. I bath my dogs maybe a couple of times a year – generally in the summer when they love to play under the hose, rarely in the winter – and I show my dogs regularly. Again, if the dog's diet and exercise regime is good, the coat should be healthy.

Eyes

The eyes may need gentle wiping with damp cotton wool (cotton) or baby wipes. If you have a white Boxer, this area will become tear-stained. This is normal, but gentle wiping may help; it will certainly stop a crusty formation and soreness. If the area looks as if it is getting sore, applying a little Vaseline through the creases will help to protect the skin.

Ears

The ears should need less attention, but it is important that you check them regularly to ensure that everything is in order. Look for signs of redness, dry and sore patches, and a dark, thick wax-like substance. Most ear issues are easily treated; it is advisable to keep an ear cleanser so you can gently wipe this delicate area, using damp cotton wool. Never use ear buds, and do not probe into the ear canal.

Mouth/teeth

Teeth should be kept healthy by a good diet and by providing hard, rubber chews and rope toys. You can give dental sticks, or you can use an additive to food to help prevent the build-up of plaque.

Routine teeth cleaning with a special canine toothpaste will help to keep teeth clean and strong. However, as with humans, some dogs are born with better, stronger teeth than others. Check regularly for signs of red, sore areas. If your dog is off his food, always examine his teeth for possible problems.

Some Boxers object to this type of handling, so get your puppy used to it from an early age.

Make sure you can put your hands alongside his teeth/jawline, and observe closely so you know what is normal for your dog. If your Boxer needs a dental check, it is important that the vet is able to assess the dog without too much fuss. A general anesthetic will be needed to remove tartar or to remove teeth. This does carry a small risk, but it's a common procedure for the vet, and the dog will normally recover very quickly.

Feet

If the feet seem red and discolored, check them for a foreign body that may have got trapped, such as a grass seed or a thorn. Sometimes these can work their way inside the skin and often cause an abscess. This will need veterinary care, with antibiotics to clear up the infection. You can bathe the foot with salt water, which may prevent further infection but will not clear up an existing one.

Keep an eye on the nails; these need to be kept short by walking out on concrete paths or by trimming or filing. If you need to trim the nails, you should accustom your Boxer to the procedure from an early age so he is comfortable with it and does not struggle.

The Boxer is a low-maintenance breed. Regular brushing is all that is needed to keep the coat in good order.

Wipe the eyes with damp cotton-wool (cotton) or baby wipes to keep them free from debris.

Clean the ears, but do not probe into the ear canal.

Nails will need to be trimmed on a regular basis.

Be careful to avoid cutting the dog's quick, as it will bleed profusely. The pink quick is easy to spot on white claws and you will need to cut just below this. Black nails are more difficult, so just take off a little at a time. If you are concerned, ask your vet or your puppy's breeder to help.

The show dog

Presenting your dog for the show ring is hugely important if you want to do well. It is so much better for a judge to see a clean and tidy dog that does not smell than to be put off by a dirty-looking dog.

The Boxer is relatively easy to prepare for the ring; there is no excessive brushing or grooming required. All you need to do is a little trimming of the stray hairs at the end of the tail to give a tidy appearance. You may also decide to trim the whiskers around the muzzle and the feathers down the back of the hind legs. Wipe the creases on the face and check the ears are clean.

Ensure that the white markings are clean, even on the feet, and then polish the coat with a sheepskin glove to give a really good finish.

Exercising your Boxer

The key to exercise is balance: a good balance between energy in and energy out, a good balance between controlled on-lead exercise and free running, and a good balance between learning and playing. Although the Boxer is an exuberant dog and loves his exercise, he must not overdo it. The result would be an over-active dog who does not hold good condition because he has run it off. So a good daily routine of feeding and exercise is required.

Swimming

Boxers love to swim. If possible, take your dog to a specialised dog swimming facility. It is good for muscle development and is beneficial if your Boxer is recovering from injury or lameness. Boxers also love to run on the beach and swim in the sea – just be sensible, and make sure there is no danger of your Boxer getting into difficulties.

Playing games

Boxers thrive on playing games, especially ones that need their mental abilities stretched as well as their bodies. Soccer is good if you can find a ball that lasts long enough! If you play retrieve games, make sure you always use safe articles. Sticks can be very dangerous, as they can damage the dog's mouth.

Facing page:
The Boxer needs an
outlet for his energy.

The older Boxer

I think the older Boxer does not need to be treated as 'old' until absolutely necessary. As long as no health problems are evident, a Boxer aged eight or nine can be very active and can be fed an adult maintenance diet. Once you start to notice some slowing down, and maybe some weight increase, change to a senior diet, which will ensure correct nutrients but not so many calories.

Try to keep to your regular exercise routine for as long as the dog is able, reducing to lead-walking if he becomes stiff and unwilling. Always ensure your older Boxer is dried off well if he gets wet and keep him warm and comfortable in a cosy bed.

Inevitably, the time comes when we have to say goodbye to our beloved Boxer. It is never an easy time, but we need to be prepared. Sometimes our dogs can be taken from us at an early age when we least expect it, due to a severe illness or an unfortunate accident. In these cases, we do not have a choice, as the decision is out of our hands.

However, if your faithful friend has lived a long life – over 10 years old is quite common for a Boxer, and some make it to 12 or 14 – then you may have to make the decision yourself. What you need to ask yourself is:

- How happy is my dog?

- How much is he able to enjoy a quality life?

- Is he able to eat?

- Can he walk out to the garden to relieve himself?

- Is he able to take any exercise?

You may have heard it said that you will know when the time is right. I believe this to be true, but that does not make it any easier. Be sure you are not keeping the dog alive for your own sake. Explain the situation to other members of the family, discuss it together if appropriate, and never exclude anyone, even the children.

Taking the pain away and relieving suffering is the last kindness you can do for your old friend. Your Boxer has given you many years of fun, laughter and loyalty – and now is the time to repay him.

Below: Be aware of the changing needs of your Boxer as he grows older.

training guidelines

As we have seen, the Boxer is a breed that requires leadership and, by training and socializing, you can help him to find his place in the family pack.

Training should never be seen as a chore. It is a fun, rewarding time you spend with your Boxer and will be the means of building a closer bond.

In order to train successfully, you need to establish some guidelines to ensure that learning is always a positive experience.

- Find a reward your Boxer values so he is motivated to work for you. More often than not, this will be a tasty treat – cheese, sausage and cooked liver are all favorites. However, some Boxers prefer a game with a toy. If this is the case, make sure you only produce the toy at training sessions so it has special value. If you are using

treats as a reward, make sure you adjust your Boxer's meals accordingly, otherwise he will soon be piling on the pounds.

- Keep training sessions short, particularly while your Boxer is young. Puppies have a limited attention span and it is far more effective to train when your pup is keen and fresh.

- Never train after a walk, a play session or a meal – your Boxer will be sadly lacking in enthusiasm.

- Choose a training area that is relatively free from distractions to help your Boxer to concentrate. It may be easier to train indoors to begin with, and add more distractions as you progress.

- Reward frequently when you are teaching a new exercise, and then reward on a random basis to keep your Boxer guessing.

- Break every exercise into small steps, and reward each stage before linking them together.

- If your Boxer is struggling with an exercise, either break it down into smaller steps (see above), or ask him to do something easy, such as a Sit or a Beg, so you can reward him and take the pressure off him.

- Never train when you are in a bad mood, or if you are short of time – the training session will be doomed to failure.

- Always end on a positive note, with your Boxer still keen and willing to work.

- Remember, training should be fun for both you, and your Boxer.

Clicker training

There are many different methods of training, and as long as the methods you use are positive and reward-based, you will not go far wrong.

You may decide you want to get involved with clicker training – a modern approach that has proved very effective. The clicker is the size of a matchbox, fitted with a small device that makes a noise when it is pressed. The puppy is taught that a 'click' means a reward will follow, so he quickly learns to work for a 'click'.

As a trainer, you need to get your timing right and 'click' at the precise moment your puppy does what you want, and then reward him. In this way, your puppy will repeat the desired behavior, knowing that he will earn a 'click' and then get a treat. I have found this method of training to be successful with Boxer puppies and older dogs alike.

It does not take a Boxer long to learn that if he earns a 'click' he gets a reward.

First lessons

Educating your Boxer begins the day you bring him home – it is the key to building a happy and successful life together.

Puppy training and socialization

Introduce your puppy to as many different people as possible, and to all the different household noises – the vacuum cleaner, the dishwasher, the television, etc. Allow him to explore your home and garden, within safe limits. The more confidence he gains in a familiar environment, the easier it will be for him once he is allowed into the outside world.

When your puppy has completed his vaccination course – remember he will not be fully protected until 10 days after his second injection – you can broaden his horizons. Find a local dog club that offers puppy socialization, or you may find that your vet runs classes. This gives your puppy the opportunity to learn how to behave with other dogs and people.

Lead walking

In order to socialize your Boxer in the outside world, you will need to teach him to walk confidently on a lead. In any case, this is best taught early on before your Boxer becomes too big and strong.

- Attach the lead and hold a treat in the hand nearest your puppy. As you walk, show the treat to your puppy so that he walks alongside you. Continue for a few paces and then reward him with the treat.

- Repeat, introducing the "Heel" command when your pup is walking in the correct position.

- Build this up in easy stages, making sure you use verbal encouragement and reward your pup at regular intervals.

Out and about

Introduce your Boxer to lots of different environments, such as the park, the local shops and the vet's surgery, allowing him time to look, to be brave and to approach different things himself.

If your puppy seems apprehensive, do not mother him, pandering to his behavior by moving away or picking him up. Take more time, talk to your puppy and show him you are not bothered by whatever seems to be the issue.

Traffic can be very scary, but your puppy must learn to tolerate it. Start off in light traffic, progressing to more challenging environments as his confidence increases. Remember: what you do in these early months will impact on your whole life together.

Come when called

This is one of the most important exercises you can teach your Boxer, and it will be of great benefit to you both. If you have a dog who reliably comes when called, you will be able to allow him far greater freedom so you can both enjoy adventurous walks together.

When using this command, a change of voice is required. You need to sound interesting and jolly; a higher-pitched voice usually works.

- Start practising in the home, calling puppy's name and then rewarding him when he comes to you. A puppy has a natural desire to follow, so capitalise on this from day one.

- At mealtimes, try calling him from one room to another – and then you will have a really worthwhile reward to give him.

- Progress to calling your puppy when he is the garden, making sure you give lots of verbal encouragement and praise him when he comes, as well as rewarding him with a treat or a game with his favorite toy.

- When you are confident that your pup is responding well at home, try recalling him from a free run. Make sure you have lots of tasty treats, and call him to you at intervals throughout the walk so that he does not think the recall means the end of his fun.

- If your puppy is slow to respond, try to make yourself irresistible! Make the "Come" command sound fun and exciting to motivate him to come back to you. If necessary jump up and down, or run off in the opposite direction, so he comes chasing after you. It doesn't matter how silly you look – as long as it works!

Do not make the mistake of reprimanding your Boxer if he is slow to come back to you. No matter, how little you feel like it, you must praise him and reward him, otherwise he will build up a bad association with the recall and will not want to come back to you in future.

Make yourself irresistible so your Boxer always wants to come back to you.

Stationary exercises

These exercises are easy to teach, and rewarding for both you and your Boxer as you can achieve almost instant success.

Sit

This can be used as a way of gaining your dog's attention, to aid control, or it can be used at a kerbside.

- When first teaching this, hold a treat above your puppy's nose, which will encourage him to move his head backwards and go into position. Reward him with the treat.

- When he is responding to the lure, use the command "Sit". Once he is in the sit position, reward with your voice and a treat.

* You can practice at mealtimes, first asking your puppy to "Sit" before you put his bowl down.

Down

This can be used as an additional control aid, and it can be useful when grooming your Boxer, or if he needs to be examined by a vet. If you can teach an instant Down, it can be a lifesaver, as you will be able to bring your Boxer to an instant halt if an emergency arises.

- Ask your puppy to "Sit" and, using a treat, move it down from your puppy's nose to the floor. This will lure the dog into position as he tries to get the treat.

- Do not give your puppy the treat until he is in the down position, then praise with your voice and give him the treat.

- When he is following the lure and going into position, introduce the "Down" command.

When your Boxer understands the verbal cue, you can start asking him to go "Down" when you are a distance from him, or put him on the lead, run a few steps and then ask him to go "Down". With practice, this will result in an instant response – even if your Boxer is running ahead of you.

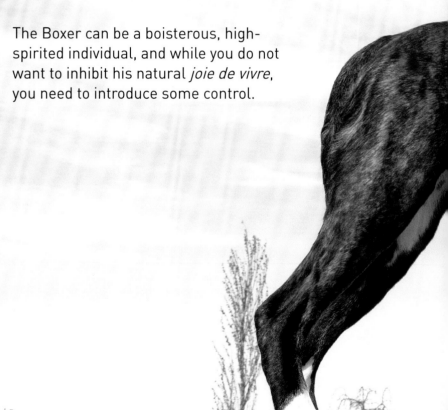

The Boxer can be a boisterous, high-spirited individual, and while you do not want to inhibit his natural *joie de vivre*, you need to introduce some control.

Wait

This command brings your dog to a temporary halt, so gain his attention before giving the next command.

- Start training this exercise at mealtimes, by asking your puppy to "Sit", and waiting a few seconds before putting down the bowl and allowing him to eat.

- Once your puppy has grasped the concept that he must "wait", transfer it to another situation, such as before you open a door, at the kerbside, or when you are opening the car door and need to clip on his lead..

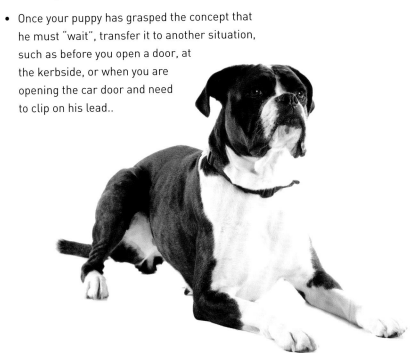

Stay

This tells your Boxer to stay in position until he is released.

This is another control aid that can be used to calm a dog and to keep him from danger. It is an extension of the Wait exercise, but you should be able to move away from the dog while he remains in position.

- Start with your puppy in the Down position, and attach a lead. Move one step away, and use a hand signal – palm held flat towards the puppy – to block his advance. Go back to him and reward him.

- Build this up step by step until your puppy will stay in position when you are some distance from him. Always go back to your puppy to reward him rather than calling him to you when the exercise is finished so he knows he must stay in position. A release word, such as "OK," can be used to tell your Boxer the exercise is finished and he is free to move.

Leave

You can use this to prevent your Boxer eating or chewing something he is not allowed, or which might be dangerous.

- Use a toy, such as a tuggy, and play with your puppy. When you decide to take the toy away, loosen your grip so the toy is no longer interesting. Show him you have a treat in your hand and ask him to "Leave" the toy.

- Reward with your voice and with treats when this is achieved.

- Keep practising so that "Leave" means let go instantly. Make sure you reward well so your Boxer learns that it is better for him if he does as you ask.

It is your job to give your Boxer the
firm, fair and consistent leadership
that is required. If you are prepared to
do this from day one, you need never
experience problems with your dog.

You need to bear in mind that an adorable puppy
that entertains you with his mischievous antics will
quickly grow into a powerful, strong-willed adult.
You do not need to bully your Boxer, but you do need
to earn his respect.

When your Boxer hits adolescence you may well see
changes in his behavior as he starts to challenge
your leadership. This is natural behavior – it is
exactly what we see among human teenagers. Your
Boxer is simply testing the boundaries to see if he
can better his position in the human pack.

It is important that you assert your own authority at the first instance. Allowing this type of behavior will be seen as acceptance, and the dog's desire to lead will grow.

Try to be non-confrontational – for example, if your Boxer growls as you approach his food bowl, drop some extra food in so he welcomes your interference. In this way, you are showing you are the provider and should be respected.

If he tries to 'guard' a toy, take all his toys away, and only let him play with a toy when he is interacting with you. Again, you are showing that you 'own' the toys, and he must play by your rules.

With sensible guidance, your Boxer will come through adolescence and mature into an outstanding family companion. Make sure you are always there for him, giving him the time and commitment he needs.

It is not sufficient to care for his physical needs alone, the ideal owner must tune into the Boxer's mind and provide leadership and security. In return, the Boxer will give you a lifetime of unconditional love and loyalty.

Facing page:
If you give your Boxer
the leadership he
requires, he will be
happy to find his place
in the family pack.

After the successful completion of puppy training classes, there are a number of options for further development. The Boxer is a highly intelligent breed and will relish the opportunity to use his brain.

Agility

Puppies should not be allowed to do any agility that involves jumping or contact equipment until at least 12 months old. But while you are waiting, you can begin to teach your dog how to weave, introduce him to tunnels, and play around colored jumps and poles so that he becomes familiar with the equipment.

Agility is judged on the time taken to get around a course, with faults given for:

- Fences knocked down.

- Obstacles missed or not completed correctly.

- Missed contact points on the A-frame, seesaw or dog-walk.

- A dog and handler are eliminated for taking the wrong course.

Agility is fast and furious and is great for the fitness of both handler and dog; it can be quite addictive! The obstacles include hurdles, long jump, tire jump, tunnels (rigid and collapsible), weaving poles, an A-frame, a dog-walk and a seesaw.

Good Citizen Scheme

The Good Citizen Scheme is run in the UK and in the USA. It promotes responsible ownership and helps you to train a well-behaved dog that will fit in with the community.

The schemes are excellent for pet owners and is also an ideal starting point if you plan to compete with your Boxer when he is older.

In the UK there are three levels – bronze, silver and gold – with each test becoming progressively more demanding. In the AKC scheme there is a single test.

Obedience

The classes start off being relatively easy and become progressively more challenging, with additional exercises and minimal instructions from the handler.

Exercises include:

- **Heelwork:** Dog and handler must complete a set pattern on and off the lead, which includes left turns, right turns, about turns, and changes of pace.

- **Recall:** This may be when the handler is stationary or on the move.

- **Retrieve:** This may be a dumbbell or any article chosen by the judge.

- **Sendaway:** The dog is sent to a designated spot and must go into an instant Down until he is recalled by the handler.

- **Stays:** The dog must stay in the Sit and in the Down for a set amount of time. In advanced classes, the handler is out of sight.

- **Scent:** The dog must retrieve a single cloth from a pre-arranged pattern of cloths that has his owner's scent, or, in advanced classes, the judge's scent. There may also be decoy cloths.

- **Distance control:** The dog must execute a series of moves (Sit, Stand, Down) without leaving his position and with the handler at a distance.

- **Agility:** In the US, agility is included with a retrieve over a jump, a long jump, and in directed jumping, where the dog must leave the handler and then, when instructed, clear the obstacle that is indicated.

Tracking/Working Trials

In the UK tracking is incorporated into working trials, which involve the additional disciplines of control and agility. In the US, however, tracking is a sport in its own right.

The Boxer was highly valued by the armed services at earlier stage in his development and he retains the ability to work closely with his handler, and on his own initiative.

Both tracking and working trails require a lot of dedication and training, but if you have the time and the patience, your Boxer will rise to the challenge.

Showing

If you decide that you would like to have a go at dog showing, this can be started at a very early age with ringcraft classes for puppies from three months old. You will need to find a local club where there are people who know how the show scene works. It is best to start at the smaller, informal shows, before moving on to bigger shows for all breeds, then breed club or specialty shows. If you are determined enough, and your dog is good enough, you can compete in Championship shows where you may even achieve the dream of making your Boxer a show Champion.

We are fortunate that the Boxer is a relatively healthy dog, with no exaggerations. With good routine care, a well-balanced diet, and sufficient exercise, most dogs will experience few health problems.

However, it is your responsibility to put a program of preventative health care in place – and this should start from the moment your puppy, or older dog, arrives in his new home.

Vaccinations

Dogs are subject to a number of contagious diseases. In the old days, these were killers, and resulted in heartbreak for many owners. Vaccinations have now been developed, and the occurrence of the major infectious diseases is now very rare. However, this will only remain the case if all pet owners follow a strict policy of vaccinating their dogs.

There are vaccinations available for the following diseases:

Adenovirus: This affects the liver; affected dogs have a classic 'blue eye'.

Distemper: A viral disease which causes chest and gastro-intestinal damage. The brain may also be affected, leading to fits and paralysis.

Parvovirus: Causes severe gastro enteritis, and most commonly affects puppies.

Leptospirosis: This bacterial disease is carried by rats and affects many mammals, including humans. It causes liver and kidney damage.

Rabies: A virus that affects the nervous system and is invariably fatal. The first signs are abnormal behavior when the infected dog may bite another animal or a person. Paralysis and death follow. Vaccination is compulsory in most countries. In the UK, dogs travelling overseas must be vaccinated.

Kennel Cough: There are several strains of Kennel Cough, but they all result in a harsh, dry, cough. This disease is rarely fatal; in fact most dogs make a good recovery within a matter of weeks and show few signs of ill health while they are affected. However, kennel cough is highly infectious among dogs that live together so, for this reason, most boarding kennels will insist that your dog is protected by the vaccine, which is given as nose drops.

Lyme Disease: This is a bacterial disease transmitted by ticks (see page 164). The first signs are limping, but the heart, kidneys and nervous system can also be affected. The ticks that transmit the disease occur in specific regions, such as the north-east states of the USA, some of the southern states, California and the upper Mississippi region. Lyme disease is till rare in the UK so vaccinations are not routinely offered.

Vaccination Program

In the USA, the American Animal Hospital Association advises vaccination for core diseases, which they list as distemper, adenovirus, parvovirus and rabies. The requirement for vaccinating for non-core diseases – leptospirosis, Lyme disease and kennel cough – should be assessed depending on a dog's individual risk and his likely exposure to the disease.

In the UK, vaccinations are routinely given for distemper, adenovirus, leptospirosis and parvovirus.

In most cases, a puppy will start his vaccinations at around eight weeks of age, with the second part given 14-28 days later. However, this does vary depending on the individual policy of veterinary practices, and the incidence of disease in your area.

You should also talk to your vet about whether to give annual booster vaccinations. This depends on an individual dog's levels of immunity, and how long a particular vaccine remains effective.

Parasites

No matter how well you look after your Boxer, you will have to accept that parasites – internal and external – are ever present, and you need to take preventative action.

Internal parasites: As the name suggests, these parasites live inside your dog. Most will find a home in the digestive tract, but there is also a parasite that lives in the heart. If infestation is unchecked, a dog's health will be severely jeopardized, but routine preventative treatment is simple and effective.

External parasites: These parasites live on your dog's body – in his skin and fur, and sometimes in his ears.

Roundworm

This is found in the small intestine. Signs of infestation will be a poor coat, a pot belly, diarrhoea and lethargy. Prospective mothers should be treated prior to mating, but it is almost inevitable that parasites will be passed on to the puppies. For this reason, a breeder will start a worming program, which you will need to continue. Ask your vet for advice on treatment, which will need to continue throughout your dog's life.

Tapeworm

Infection occurs when fleas and lice are ingested; the adult worm takes up residence in the small intestine, releasing mobile segments (which contain eggs) which can be seen in a dog's feces as small rice-like grains. The only other obvious sign of infestation is irritation of the anus. Again, routine preventative treatment is required throughout your Boxer's life.

Heartworm

This parasite is transmitted by mosquitoes, and so is more likely to be present in areas with a warm, humid climate. However, it is found in all parts of the USA, although its prevalence does vary. At present, heartworm is rarely seen in the UK.

Heartworms live in the right side of the heart and larvae can grow up to 14 in (35 cm) in length. A dog with heartworm is at severe risk from heart failure, so preventative treatment, as advised by your vet, is essential. Dogs living in the USA should also have regular tests to check for the presence of infection.

Lungworm

Lungworm, or *Angiostrongylus vasorum*, is a parasite that lives in the heart and major blood vessels supplying the lungs. It can cause many problems, such as breathing difficulties, excessive bleeding, sickness, diarrhoea, seizures, and even death. The dog becomes infected when ingesting slugs and snails, often accidentally when rummaging through undergrowth. Lungworm is not common, but it is on the increase and a responsible owner should be aware of it. Fortunately, it is easily preventable and even affected dogs usually make a full recovery if treated early enough. Your vet will be able to advise you on the risks in your area and what form of treatment may be required.

Fleas

A dog may carry dog fleas, cat fleas, and even human fleas. The flea stays on the dog only long enough to feed and breed, but its presence will result in itching. If your dog has an allergy to fleas – usually a reaction to the flea's saliva – he will scratch himself until he is raw. Spot-on treatment, which should be administered on a routine basis, is easy to use and highly effective. You can also treat your dog with a spray or with insecticidal shampoo. Bear in mind that your dog's whole environment and all other pets in your home will also need to be treated.

How to detect fleas

You may suspect your dog has fleas, but how can you be sure? There are two methods to try.

Run a fine comb through your dog's coat, and see if you can detect the presence of fleas on the skin, or clinging to the comb. Alternatively, sit your dog on some white paper and rub his back. This will dislodge feces from the fleas, which will be visible as small brown specks. To double check, shake the specks on to some damp cotton wool (cotton). Flea feces consists of the dried blood taken from the host, so if the specks turn a lighter shade of red, you know your dog has fleas.

Ticks

These are blood-sucking parasites which are most frequently found in rural area where sheep or deer are present.

The main danger is their ability to pass Lyme disease to both dogs and humans. Lyme disease is prevalent in some areas of the USA (see page 157), although it is still rare in the UK. The treatment you give your dog for fleas generally works for ticks, but you should discuss the best product to use with your veterinary surgeon.

How to remove a tick

If you spot a tick on your dog, do not try to pluck it off as you risk leaving the hard mouth parts embedded in his skin. The best way to remove a tick is to use a fine pair of tweezers or you can buy a tick remover. Grasp the tick head firmly and then pull the tick straight out from the skin. If you are using a tick remover, check the instructions, as some recommend a circular twist when pulling. When you have removed the tick, clean the area with mild soap and water.

Ear mites

These parasites live in the outer ear canal. The signs of infestation are a brown, waxy discharge, and your dog will continually shake his head and scratch his ear.

If you suspect your Boxer has ear mites, a visit to the vet will be needed so that medicated ear drops can be prescribed.

Fur mites

These small, white parasites are visible to the naked eye and are often referred to as 'walking dandruff'. They cause a scurfy coat and mild itchiness. However, they are zoonotic – transferable to humans – so prompt treatment with an insecticide prescribed by your vet is essential.

Harvest mites

These are picked up from the undergrowth, and can be seen as a bright orange patch on the webbing between the toes, although this can be found elsewhere on the body, such as on the ear flaps. Treatment is effective with the appropriate insecticide, prescribed by your vet.

Skin mites

There are two types of parasite that burrow into a dog's skin. Demodex canis is transferred from a mother to her pups while they are feeding. Treatment is with a topical preparation, and sometimes antibiotics are needed. Refer to your vet.

The other skin mite is sarcoptes scabiei, which causes intense itching and hair loss. It is highly contagious, so all dogs in a household will need to be treated, which involves repeated bathing with a medicated shampoo.

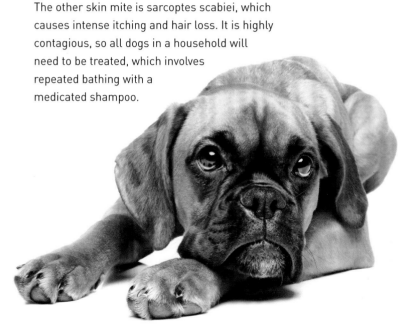

Below: Regular grooming will ensure you detect the presence of parasites.

Common ailments

As with all living animals, dogs can be affected by a variety of ailments, most of which can be treated effectively after consulting with your vet, who will prescribe appropriate medication and will advise you on how to care for your dog's needs.

Here are some of the more common problems that could affect your Boxer, with advice on how to deal with them.

Anal glands

These are two small sacs on either side of the anus, which produce a dark-brown secretion that dogs use when they mark their territory. The anal glands should empty every time a dog defecates but, if they become blocked or impacted, a dog will experience increasing discomfort. He may nibble at his rear end,

or 'scoot' his bottom along the ground to relieve the irritation.

Treatment involves a trip to the vet who will empty the glands manually. It is important to do this without delay or infection may occur.

Dental problems

Good dental hygiene will do much to minimize problems with gum infection and tooth decay. If tartar accumulates to the extent that you cannot remove it by brushing, the vet will need to intervene. In a situation such as this, an anesthetic will need to be administered so the tartar can be removed manually.

Diarrhoea

There are many reasons why a dog has diarrhoea, but most commonly it is the result of scavenging, a sudden change of diet, or an adverse reaction to a particular type of food.

If your dog is suffering from diarrhoea, the first step is to withdraw food for a day. It is important that he does not dehydrate, so make sure that fresh drinking water is available. However, drinking too much can increase the diarrhoea, which may be accompanied with vomiting, so limit how much he drinks at any one time.

Facing page:
Eating unsuitable
foods can cause
digestive problems.

After allowing the stomach to rest, feed a bland diet, such as white fish or chicken with boiled rice for a few days. In most cases, your dog's motions will return to normal and you can resume normal feeding, although this should be done gradually.

However, if this fails to work and the diarrhoea persists for more than a few days, you should consult you vet. Your dog may have an infection, which needs to be treated with antibiotics, or the diarrhoea may indicate some other problem which needs expert diagnosis.

Ear Infections

The Boxer's ears lie close to his head in dogs that have not been cropped, so air cannot circulate as freely as it would in a dog with cropped ears. However, regardless of whether your Boxer has cropped or uncropped ears, it is important to check them on a routine basis.

A healthy ear is clean with no sign of redness or inflammation, and no evidence of a waxy brown discharge or a foul odor. If you see your dog scratching his ear, shaking his head, or holding one ear at an odd angle, you will need to consult your vet.

The most likely causes are ear mites (see page 166), an infection, or there may a foreign body, such as a grass seed, trapped in the ear.

Depending on the cause, treatment is with medicated ear drops, possibly containing antibiotics. If a foreign body is suspected, the vet will need to carry our further investigations.

Eye Problems

The Boxer's eyes are round and forward facing, but they should not protrude, which would make them vulnerable to injury.

However, if your Boxer's eyes look red and sore, he may be suffering from conjunctivitis. This may, or may not be accompanied with a watery or a crusty discharge. Conjunctivitis can be caused by a bacterial or viral infection, it could be the result of an injury, or it could be an adverse reaction to pollen.

You will need to consult your vet for a correct diagnosis, but in the case of an infection, treatment with medicated eye drops is effective.

Conjunctivitis may also be the first sign of more serious inherited eye problems, see page 183.

Foreign bodies

In the home, puppies – and some older dogs – cannot resist chewing anything that looks interesting. The Boxer can be quite destructive, so the toys you choose should be suitably robust to

Facing page:
The Boxer's eyes
should be bright and
sparkling with no
sign of soreness or
discharge.

withstand damage. It is all too easy for a Boxer to bite off bits of rubber and plastic, which are highly indigestible and could cause an obstruction in his intestine. This is potentially lethal.

The signs to look for are vomiting, and a tucked up posture. The dog will often be restless and will look as though he is in pain. In this situation, you must get your dog to the vet without delay as surgery will be needed to remove the obstruction.

The other type of foreign body that may cause problems is grass seed. A grass seed can enter an orifice such as a nostril, down an ear, the gap between the eye and the eyelid, or it can penetrate the soft skin between the toes. It can also be swallowed.

The introduction of a foreign body induces a variety of symptoms, depending on the point of entry and where it travels to. The signs to look for include head shaking/ear scratching, the eruption of an abscess, sore, inflamed eyes, or a persistent cough. The vet will be able to make a proper diagnosis, and surgery may be required.

Heatstroke

The Boxer is a brachycephalic breed with a short muzzle and a flat nose, which means that breathing may require more effort than it is does in other breeds. For this reason, his cooling system is not so efficient and he is therefore more susceptible to heatstroke.

When the temperature rises, make sure your dog always has access to shady areas, and wait for a cooler part of the day before going for a walk. Be extra careful if you leave your Boxer in the car, as the temperature can rise dramatically even on a cloudy day. Heatstroke can happen very rapidly, and unless you are able lower your dog's temperature, it can be fatal.

If your Boxer appears to be suffering from heatstroke, lie him flat and then cool him as quickly as possible by hosing him, covering him with wet towels, or using frozen food bags from the freezer. As soon as he has made some recovery, take him to the vet where cold intravenous fluids can be administered.

Lameness/ Limping

There are a wide variety of reasons why a dog can go lame, from a simple muscle strain to a fracture, ligament damage, or more complex problems with the joints which may be an inherited disorder (see pages 186). It takes an expert to make a correct diagnosis, so if you are concerned about your dog, do not delay in seeking help.

As your Boxer becomes elderly, he may suffer from arthritis, which you will see as general stiffness, particularly when he gets up after resting. It will help if you ensure his bed is in a warm, draught-free location, and, if your Boxer gets wet after exercise, you must dry him thoroughly.

If your elderly Boxer seems to be in pain, consult your vet who will be able to help with pain relief medication.

Skin Problems

The Boxer is prone to a number of skin conditions so you should check him thoroughly at grooming sessions and watch out for excessive scratching or nibbling at the skin.

The first step is to make sure your Boxer is free from fleas. There are other external parasites which cause itching and hair loss, but you will need a vet to help you find the culprit.

An allergic reaction can also result in skin problems. Your Boxer may be suffering from either:

Atopy: This is an inherited predisposition to develop a hypersensitivity to environmental allergens (e.g. pollens, dust mites, moulds). Initial signs are localized licking, itching and reddening of skin and may progress to generalized self-trauma, secondary infection, scaling and crusting.

Treatment can involve steroids, antibiotics and even desensitisation vaccines following skin testing to determine the causative allergen.

Food hypersensitivity: Boxers can also have reactions to allergens in food. This may result in chronic diarrhoea, intolerance of certain foods, itchy skin or sore ears. The clinical signs often vary in severity and diagnosis involves lengthy and strict food trials.

For information on breed disposed skin disorders, see page 187.

Inherited disorders

The Boxer does have a few breed-related disorders, and if diagnosed with any of the diseases listed below, it is important to remember that they can affect offspring so breeding from affected dogs should be discouraged.

There are now recognized screening tests to enable breeders to check for affected individuals and hence reduce the prevalence of these diseases within the breed. These include schemes run by the British Veterinary Association, Kennel Club and International Sheep Dog Society in the UK, or the Orthopedic Foundation for Animals and Canine Eye Registration Foundation in the US. DNA testing is also becoming more widely available, and as research into the different genetic diseases progresses, more DNA tests are being developed.

Cancers

There are many types of skin tumor affecting Boxers. Often they can be surgically removed, thereby preventing spread if treated early enough. If you notice any lumps or abnormality in the skin or coat of your dog then you should visit your veterinary surgeon as soon as possible.

Malignant lymphoma is a cancer of lymphocyte cells (white blood cells) and is seen at a higher incidence in Boxers. Occasionally, chemotherapy may be carried out to increase life expectancy.

We still know very little about the cause of cancer and so if you are getting a puppy, you should ask the breeder about cancer in the breeding line.

Eye conditions

There is one eye condition that particularly affects Boxers. The Boxer is predisposed to Refractory Corneal Ulceration (also known as Indolent Ulcer or Boxer Ulcer), which results in slow-healing ulcers often found in both eyes. Initial signs are a painful, reddened eye with excess amounts of clear or colored discharge. These signs worsen without treatment and will ultimately result in permanent damage to the eye.

Corneal dystrophy (abnormality of the epithelium of the cornea) makes the Boxer eye susceptible to these ulcers, as it affects the normal healing process required to cope with trauma. This abnormality also enables ulcers to occur spontaneously without previous trauma. Indolent ulcers are typically difficult to treat with medication alone, may require surgery and often recur.

Gastric dilation/volvulus

This condition, commonly known as bloat or gastric torsion, is where the stomach swells visibly (dilatation) and then rotates (volvulus), so that the exit into the small intestine becomes blocked, preventing food from leaving. This results in stomach pain and a bloated abdomen. It is a severe, life-threatening condition that requires immediate veterinary attention (usually surgery) to decompress and return the stomach to its normal position.

There appears to be several risk factors causing the development of GDV and by taking the following precautions, you can reduce the risk.

- Feed two smaller meals per day instead one large one.

- Do not allow the dog to drink a large volume of water at one time.

- Do not feed immediately before or after strenuous exercise – wait at least two hours.

Heart disease

Heart disease has been a problem in the breed,with a couple of conditions that affect Boxers.

Aortic Stenosis

This is a hereditary disease, but testing of breeding stock is now doing much to reduce its incidence. This condition affects the aortic valve in the heart. Narrowing of the valve causes a murmur (graded 0-6) to be heard on cardiac auscultation as the blood is pushed through at a faster velocity than normal. This increased effort needed to push the blood through results in an increase in size of the left ventricle muscle of the heart as the muscle works harder.

Diagnosis involves Doppler echocardiography, which can determine the flow rate of the blood through the valves of the heart. Boxers with mild forms of AS can show no clinical signs. More severe forms are usually degenerative and heart failure will occur as the heart loses the ability to cope. Restricted exercise may help slow progression of the disease and medications can be prescribed to help the heart efficacy.

All breeding stock should be tested by a qualified cardiologist before matings are planned.

Boxer Arrhythmogenic Right Ventricular Cardiomyopathy

This is a genetic disease that appears to run in family lines and causes ventricular premature complexes (irregular beats) of the heart in the adult dog. There may also be enlargement of the right side chambers of the heart and reduced efficiency of the heart pump, resulting in congestive heart failure. Clinical signs include coughing or breathlessness, exercise intolerance, collapse and sudden death.

Diagnosis usually involves initial blood sampling and X-rays, then an ECG (electrocardiography) and echocardiography (ultrasound) of the heart. A Holtor monitor to measure each heartbeat over 24 hours can be useful in diagnosing the severity of the disease.

Treatment is aimed at slowing the progression of the disease and controlling the clinical signs with daily medication.

Hip dysplasia (HD)

This is where the ball and socket joint of the hip develops incorrectly so that the head of the femur (ball) and the acetabulum of the pelvis (socket) do not fit snugly. This causes pain in the joint and may be seen as lameness in dogs as young as five months old with deterioration into severe arthritis over time. Gentle exercise, reduction in obesity, anti-inflammatory drugs and home management are all part of the treatment regimes.

In the UK X-rays are sent to the British Veterinary Association, whereas in the US X-rays are submitted to the Orthopedic Foundation for Animals, where they are graded according to the risk of hip dysplasia. Severely affected dogs should not be used for breeding.

Skin disorders

The Boxer has a sensitive skin and may suffer from the following disorders:

Muzzle furunculosis

Also known as canine acne, this presents as comedones (blackheads) and can progress to pustules and papules (infected spots) on the skin of the muzzle, which may be irritating and can become infected. Generally this is a self-limiting disease, but if infected or irritating, treatment in the form of shampoo or antibiotics may be indicated.

Pododermatitis

This is inflammation of the skin of the feet and can have many initiating factors. Often your Boxer will be seen excessively licking or nibbling at reddened or inflamed areas, which can complicate the disease process. Regular bathing and antibiotic treatment are often necessary to control clinical signs.

Estrogen responsive dermatosis

A rare condition found in neutered female Boxers, resulting in bilateral symmetrical alopecia (hair loss).

Canine follicular dysplasia

Abnormal development of the hair follicles results in coat changes and alopecia. Boxers can suffer from a form that waxes and wanes with the weather seasons, resulting in alopecia on both flanks.

Truncal solar dermatitis

This is more commonly seen in white-haired Boxers where the depigmentation of the skin predisposes it to damage from the sun. Papules and crusting occur with secondary infections. Topical and oral medications can help, but preventing exposure of the skin to sun rays is the best way to prevent damage.

Summing up

It may give the pet owner cause for concern to find out about health problems that may affect their dog, but acquiring some basic knowledge is an asset, as it will allow you to spot signs of trouble at an early stage. Early diagnosis is very often the means to the most effective treatment.

The Boxer as a breed is an energetic and bounding dog with a zest for life and will be a companion that will bring many happy memories in the years you will spend together.

Useful Addresses

Breed Kennel Clubs

Please contact your Kennel Club to obtain contact information about breed clubs in your area.

UK

The Kennel Club (UK)
1 Clarges Street London, W1J 8AB
Telephone: 0870 606 6750
Fax: 0207 518 1058
Web: www.thekennelclub.org.uk

USA

American Kennel Club (AKC)
5580 Centerview Drive, Raleigh, NC 27606.
Telephone: 919 233 9767
Fax: 919 233 3627
Email: info@akc.org
Web: www.akc.org

United Kennel Club (UKC)
100 E Kilgore Rd, Kalamazoo,
MI 49002-5584, USA.
Tel: 269 343 9020
Fax: 269 343 7037
Web: www.ukcdogs.com

Australia

Australian National Kennel Council (ANKC)
The Australian National Kennel Council is the administrative body for pure breed canine affairs in Australia. It does not, however, deal directly with dog exhibitors, breeders or judges. For information pertaining to breeders, clubs or shows, please contact the relevant State or Territory Body.

International

Fédération Cynologique Internationalé (FCI)
Place Albert 1er, 13, B-6530 Thuin, Belgium.
Tel: +32 71 59.12.38
Fax: +32 71 59.22.29
Web: www.fci.be

Training and behavior

UK

Association of Pet Dog Trainers
Telephone: 01285 810811
Web: www.apdt.co.uk

Association of Pet Behaviour Counsellors
Telephone: 01386 751151
Web: www.apbc.org.uk

USA

Association of Pet Dog Trainers
Tel: 1 800 738 3647
Web: www.apdt.com

American College of Veterinary Behaviorists
Web: www.dacvb.org

American Veterinary Society of Animal Behavior
Web: www.avsabonline.org

Australia

APDT Australia Inc
Web: www.apdt.com.au

Canine Behavior
For details of regional behaviourists, contact the relevant State or Territory Controlling Body.

Activities

UK
Agility Club
Web: www.agilityclub.co.uk

British Flyball Association
Telephone: 01628 829623
Web: www.flyball.org.uk

USA
North American Dog Agility Council
Web: www.nadac.com

North American Flyball Association, Inc.
Tel/Fax: 800 318 6312
Web: www.flyball.org

Australia
Agility Dog Association of Australia
Tel: 0423 138 914
Web: www.adaa.com.au

NADAC Australia
Web: www.nadacaustralia.com

Australian Flyball Association
Tel: 0407 337 939
Web: www.flyball.org.au

International
World Canine Freestyle Organisation
Tel: (718) 332-8336
Web: www.worldcaninefreestyle.org

Health

UK
British Small Animal Veterinary Association
Tel: 01452 726700
Web: www.bsava.com

Royal College of Veterinary Surgeons
Tel: 0207 222 2001
Web: www.rcvs.org.uk

www.dogbooksonline.co.uk/healthcare

Alternative Veterinary Medicine Centre
Tel: 01367 710324
Web: www.alternativevet.org

USA
American Veterinary Medical Association
Tel: 800 248 2862
Web: www.avma.org

American College of Veterinary Surgeons
Tel: 301 916 0200
Toll Free: 877 217 2287
Web: www.acvs.org

Canine Eye Registration Foundation
The Veterinary Medical DataBases
1717 Philo Rd, PO Box 3007,
Urbana, IL 61803-3007
Tel: 217-693-4800
Fax: 217-693-4801
Web: www.vmdb.org/cerf.html

Orthopaedic Foundation of Animals
2300 E Nifong Boulevard
Columbia, Missouri, 65201-3806
Tel: 573 442-0418
Fax: 573 875-5073
Web: www.offa.org

American Holistic Veterinary Medical
Association
Tel: 410 569 0795
Web: www.ahvma.org

Australia
Australian Small Animal Veterinary
Association
Tel: 02 9431 5090
Web: www.asava.com.au

Australian Veterinary Association
Tel: 02 9431 5000
Web: www.ava.com.au

Australian College Veterinary Scientists
Tel: 07 3423 2016
Web: www.acvsc.org.au

Australian Holistic Vets
Web: www.ahv.com.au